I0159017

Leaders Guide For Retirement Roots

RetirementRoots.org

Copyright © 2020
Retirement Project

ISBN-13: 978-1-951915-10-0

All Rights Reserved

No part of this book may be copied, used, or
reproduced without the express written consent
from the authors or publisher.

Table of Contents

Introduction 1

Session *1* 3

Session *2* 6

Session *3* 12

Session *4* 15

Session 5 17

Session *6* 22

About The Author 25

Introduction:

This study was written to help people see retirement from a completely different picture – from a God centered approach rather than a self-centered one.

As a leader it's important to understand several things. First, retirement can be an emotionally charged topic. People have very different ideas and philosophies as to what it means and will look and feel like.

The goal of this study is to completely focus on the non-financial side. When inviting people, I would encourage you to emphasize this non-financial aspect since dealing with the financial side of retirement planning may cause people to hesitate or decline participation. Therefore, discussing how much to save, where to invest, or when to take social security for example, will <u>not</u> be discussed.

Along those lines, it's also important to point out that retirement is a big decision, and some people may stress and worry about making such a big commitment. As a result, people really enjoy hearing what others may be thinking and feeling about the situation as well. This makes the study ideal for both small groups and larger workshop formats. As a group leader, engaging people in their thoughts and feelings on the various non-financial topics is essential to the success of the program.

The program is broken into six separate videos: Session 1-6

Leaders have the flexibility to break the program into as many sessions as desired. It can be a full six-week study, used as a shorter 3-week program, and for larger audiences and groups turned into a one-day, intensive program as well.

The leaders guide will focus on a six-week program. Obviously, to shorten the program, additional sessions would be grouped together.

Overview:

Instead of planning for retirement solely from a numbers-based approach, we have the opportunity to incorporate God's Word and His promises into our life after work.

Opening Discussion:

What does retirement mean to you? What is different about your retirement thoughts and plan as compared to that of your parents / grandparents?

Watch Video: 7:58

Discussion:

How does society perceive retirement, and does the Bible passage in our reading (Numbers 8:23-26) agree or disagree with that perception?

What would happen if God retired?

Consider:

- Abraham made a transition late in life after being relocated by God.
- Daniel was betrayed by his colleagues and survived a hostile takeover.
- Paul changed employers and roles, accepting a much higher risk-to-reward ratio.

Are there other characters of the Bible that can offer retirement insights or wisdom?

What does the term "Christian retirement" mean to you, and what actions, beliefs, or values support such a concept?

What impact or influence does today's Church have on the concept of retirement?

Additional Verses to Read, Reflect and Discuss:

Proverbs 13:22
[22] A good person leaves an inheritance for their children's children, but a sinner's wealth is stored up for the righteous.

Psalm 92:12-14
[12] The righteous will flourish like a palm tree, they will grow like a cedar of Lebanon;[13] planted in the house of the LORD, they will flourish in the courts of our God. [14] They will still bear fruit in old age, they will stay fresh and green,

Luke 12:16-21
[16] And he told them this parable: "The ground of a certain rich man yielded an abundant harvest. [17] He thought to himself, 'What shall I do? I have no place to store my crops.' [18] "Then he said, 'This is what I'll do. I will tear down my barns and build bigger ones, and there I will store my surplus grain. [19] And I'll say to myself, "You

have plenty of grain laid up for many years. Take life easy; eat, drink and be merry."' **20** "But God said to him, 'You fool! This very night your life will be demanded from you. Then who will get what you have prepared for yourself?' **21** "This is how it will be with whoever stores up things for themselves but is not rich toward God." Do Not Worry: **22** Then Jesus said to his disciples: "Therefore I tell you, do not worry about your life, what you will eat; or about your body, what you will wear.

Next Session we will cover Chapter 2 and complete the Retirement Perception Quiz as well as discuss Chapter 3 's The Dark Side of Retirement.

Session 2: Retirement Perceptions & Darkside of Retirement

Overview Part 1:

A key part of managing a major life transition like retirement is to have realistic ideas and expectations about what life after work may look and feel like.

Opening Discussion:

Retirement is often portrayed as the holy grail of life... the time where everything comes together and works out for the better. What are your thoughts and feelings about this perspective?

Watch Video: 9:27

Discussion:

Why do retirees struggle during their transition into this new phase of life?

What can God provide to retirees that financial security and increased leisure time do not?

If someone told you, "Don't ever retire because you won't mean anything to anyone, anymore", what would be your immediate response and why?

While retirement may offer some relief, what areas of stress may continue with us into our later years?

What may cause fear and anxiety in retirement?

How can we find or maintain our purpose in retirement?

Why is it important to take care of our health and keep a positive attitude?

What can we do to maintain our social circles?

How important is peace to overall health and wellness in retirement?

Additional Verses to Read, Reflect and Discuss:

Proverbs 12:25
[25] Anxiety weighs down the heart, but a kind word cheers it up.

Luke 12:29-31
[29] And do not set your heart on what you will eat or drink; do not worry about it. [30] For the pagan world runs after all such things, and your Father knows that you need them. [31] But seek his kingdom, and these things will be given to you as well.

John 14:27
[27] Peace I leave with you; my peace I give you. I do not give to you as the world gives. Do not let your hearts be troubled and do not be afraid.

Philippians 4:4-7

[4] Rejoice in the Lord always. I will say it again: Rejoice! [5] Let your gentleness be evident to all. The Lord is near. [6] Do not be anxious about anything, but in every situation, by prayer and petition, with thanksgiving, present your requests to God. [7] And the peace of God, which transcends all understanding, will guard your hearts and your minds in Christ Jesus.

This section is not covered in the videos but should be discussed

Overview Part 2:
You will be aware of the potential pitfalls of retirement and the strength we have in Christ to be overcomers.

Highlight Key Parts of the Chapter:
Just as God has a plan for your retirement so too does the devil. One where the bondage of addiction, the hollowness of depression, and even the fiery depths of suicide can consume retirees

- A 2020 estimate suggested that the number of retirees with alcohol and other drug problems will leap 150% to 4.4 million – up from 1.7 million in 2001.

- The National Institutes of Health report that, of the 35 million Americans age 65 or older, about two million suffer from full-blown depression. Another five million suffer from less severe forms of the illness.

- Suicide is the 11th leading cause of death in the United States, with an aggregate rate of 11 suicide deaths per 100,000 Americans.

Suicide rates are highest among people over the age of 65, according to the American Association of Suicidology (AAS). That age group makes up 12.5% of the population and accounts for 15.9% of all suicides.

- Today's seniors are from a generation that stressed self-reliance: A trait characterized by a reluctance to discuss financial and/or personal health matters. This attribute, reinforced by scientific research, suggests that contemporary seniors tend to blame themselves for their illnesses, don't want to be a burden on family, and worry that treatment will be too costly.

Discussion:

How are some of the issues we face in our lives exacerbated by retirement?

What may increase the likelihood of struggling with depression in retirement?

Why is suicide such an increased risk for retirees?

Why do people feel the need to condemn themselves for their health condition?

What are some ways can prepare for unforeseen health emergencies?

Who would you turn to for support and encouragement in times of turmoil?

How can God be involved in our retirement and help us face challenges successfully?

Additional Verses to Read, Reflect and Discuss:

Proverbs 7:25-26
25 Do not let your heart turn to her ways or stray into her paths. **26** Many are the victims she has brought down; her slain are a mighty throng

Isaiah 41:13
13 For I am the LORD your God who takes hold of your right hand and says to you, Do not fear; I will help you

1 Corinthians 10:13
13 No temptation has overtaken you except what is common to mankind. And God is faithful; he will not let you be tempted beyond what you can bear. But when you are tempted, he will also provide a way out so that you can endure it.

Next week we will cover Chapter 4 and complete the Retirement Foundations Exercise.

This can be an emotionally charged exercise that may take or require additional time, prayer, and discussion.

Overview:
You will be able to evaluate what is truly important to you about retirement and begin to align those thoughts and feelings with God word and values.

Opening Discussion:
When did you first start thinking about and planning for retirement? Were your initial goals to retire early, move to a foreign country, or live a certain way? How have those visions changed over time?

Watch Video: 16:51

Discussion:

What vision do you have for your retirement, and does that align with God's plans and promises?

What are some of the intangibles that add quality and value to our lives?

What does the "perfect" retirement look like, and how does that fit into the lives of those closest to you?

How would a sudden change in health, finances, or material wealth, change a person's vision of retirement?

What are examples of some events that may alter your retirement or planning for retirement?

How does the concept of "post-retirement legacy" change your retirement planning?

How would we change our retirement plans to focus on the things and people most important to us?

Additional Verses to Read, Reflect and Discuss:

Galatians 6:2
2 Carry each other's burdens, and in this way you will fulfill the law of Christ.

Philippians 4:12-13
12 I know what it is to be in need, and I know what it is to have plenty. I have learned the secret of being content in any and every situation, whether well fed or hungry, whether living in plenty or in want. **13** I can do all this through him who gives me strength.

1 Peter 5:10

[10] And the God of all grace, who called you to his eternal glory in Christ, after you have suffered a little while, will himself restore you and make you strong, firm and steadfast.

Philippians 3:8

[8] What is more, I consider everything a loss because of the surpassing worth of knowing Christ Jesus my Lord, for whose sake I have lost all things. I consider them garbage, that I may gain Christ

Next Session we will cover Chapter 5 and complete the Retirement Curious List and Friend List

Session 4: Curious List and Friends List

Overview:
Attendees will reconsider how to replace their work identity and sense of purpose in retirement.

Opening Discussion:
How will you introduce yourself when you are retired? What will you miss from work / career? What is one creative, out-of-the-box thing you want to do with your time in retirement?

Watch 1ˢᵗ Section of Video (Curious List): 5:05

Discussion:
How does your pre-retirement identity impact the transition into retirement roles and relationships?

What emotions and issues can develop from losing one's identity and sense of direction?

How can your natural curiosity be used to impact your retirement in a positive way?

Watch 2nd Section of Video (Friend List): 5:48

Discussion:

How could retirement disrupt our social lives and sense of being?

How can Christian people have a positive impact in relationships, especially in retirement?

What can you do to make the most of your curiosity list to build stronger relationships?

Why is it important to analyze our own attributes when assessing our relationships?

Additional Verses to Read, Reflect and Discuss:

Proverbs 17:17
17 A friend loves at all times, and a brother is born for a time of adversity.

Proverbs 27:17
17 As iron sharpens iron, so one person sharpens another.

Hebrews 10:24-25
24 And let us consider how we may spur one another on toward love and good deeds, **25** not giving up meeting together, as some are in the habit of doing, but encouraging one another— and all the more as you see the day approaching.

Ephesians 4:2-3
2 Be completely humble and gentle; be patient, bearing with one another in love. **3** Make every effort to keep the unity of the Spirit through the bond of peace.

Next session will be on Retirement Well-being

Overview:

Attendees will understand that their ability to prosper in their retirement years is dependent on keeping our bodies, mind and spirit healthy. They will develop a plan to either develop or maintain several health-related habits and opportunities to support their God-centered life in retirement.

Opening Discussion:

How are you currently preparing your body, mind, and spirit for life in retirement? How can factors like shame, guilt, and regret impact one's life in retirement?

Watch Video: 8:05

Discussion:

How could your existing lifestyle affect your health in retirement?

What reasonable changes could you make to your lifestyle to improve your general and functional health?

What are some resources you could to draw upon to maintain or make positive changes to your health?

How could your physical health and change in lifestyle affect your emotional health?
In what ways could you balance your retirement goals with your state of health?

What are some activities or interests you plan to pursue in retirement that would require good functional health?

What value does God place upon our overall health, even for those later in life?

Additional Verses to Read, Reflect and Discuss:

John 1:2
2 He was with God in the beginning.

Corinthians 6:12
12 "I have the right to do anything," you say—but not everything is beneficial. "I have the right to do anything"—but I will not be mastered by anything.

1 Timothy 4:8
8 For physical training is of some value, but godliness has value for all things, holding promise for both the present life and the life to come.

This section is not covered in the video but should be discussed in this session

Overview:

You will develop strategies to effectively discuss and communicate about your retirement planning.

Highlight Key Parts of the Chapter:

- Everyday life in retirement comes with its own stereotypes and assumptions. People may imagine how it's going to work, but aren't always   effective in communicating those thoughts, which is exactly where danger lurks.

- Words are powerful, so be mindful of what you say and how you say it during these discussions. Differing views and opinions can intensify matters and make your time in retirement tense and emotionally draining. Therefore, be patient, and be sure to seek God before having any of these discussions.

- It's important to point out that you do not have to go through and answer every single question. The goal was to develop an extensive list that you could use to identify important topics and areas that you may not have thought about before.

How do preconceptions about retirement impact the conversations we have with others?

Who are some of the people you consider stakeholders in your retirement planning?

Why is it important to have discussions about your pre-retirement identity as you plan to transition?

How could relationships change in and outside of the home in retirement, and are there relationships that *need* to change?

What are some of the ways financial obligations may change in retirement, and with whom should you have those conversations?

How do you plan to build upon your faith life in retirement, and what role would your church/fellowship play in those plans?

What changes do you hope to make to your health in retirement, and with whom (including professionals and experts) will you consult?

Additional Verses to Read, Reflect and Discuss:

Proverbs 15:22
²² Plans fail for lack of counsel, but with many advisers they succeed.

Proverbs 25:11
¹¹ Like apples of gold in settings of silver is a ruling rightly given.

Luke 14:28
²⁸ "Suppose one of you wants to build a tower. Won't you first sit down and estimate the cost to see if you have enough money to complete it?"

James 3:2
² We all stumble in many ways. Anyone who is never at fault in what they say is perfect, able to keep their whole body in check.

Next Session we wrap up and bring everything today with a Christian Retirement Plan

Overview:

You will develop a plan for retirement that incorporates God's plans and promises.

Opening Discussion:

We have covered retirement perceptions, the dark side of retirement, foundations, a curious list, friend list, well-being exercise, and retirement conversations. What has been the most eye-opening part of the program for you thus far? What have you learned or how has your thinking been validated?

Watch Video: 10:44

Discussion:

How were we able to use the various exercises to reorient your thinking about retirement?

What are some concepts you can easily communicate to others about how you view retirement?

In what ways did God become more involved in your retirement planning?

How can we become more involved in God's plans by reconsidering how we approach retirement?

Why is it important to re-evaluate your financial plans now that you have re-examined your perspective on retirement?

What are your overall goals for retirement, and did those significantly change during this course?

How can you have a positive impact on the retirement plans of a friend or family member?

Additional Verses to Read, Reflect and Discuss:

2 Corinthians 5:17
[17] Therefore, if anyone is in Christ, the new creation has come:[a] The old has gone, the new is here!

James 1:5
[5] If any of you lacks wisdom, you should ask God, who gives generously to all without finding fault, and it will be given to you.

Romans 8:31
[31] What, then, shall we say in response to these things? If God is for us, who can be against us?

1 Corinthians 15:58
[58] Therefore, my dear brothers and sisters, stand firm. Let nothing move you. Always give yourselves fully to the work of the Lord, because you know that your labor in the Lord is not in vain.

Bonus Discussion: Bloopers and Outtakes

Retirement doesn't always go as planned and the same can be said for filming a video series like this… and as we know from 1 Peter 5:6

"Humble yourselves, therefore, under God's mighty hand, that He may lift you up."

Watch Bloopers Video: 1:55

As a group, feel free to discuss some funny bloopers you've had in life, what you learned from them, and how being prepared to laugh at yourself in retirement can help.

We hope you have enjoyed the session and encourage you to provide any comments and feedback at RetirementRoots.org/contact

About The Author

Robert Laura is a pioneer in the psychology and social science of retirement planning and is a highly sought after presenter at retirement conferences and meetings across the country. He is a three-time best-selling author and nationally syndicated columnist for Forbes.com, Financial Advisor Magazine, and NextAvenue.org.

His work has reached millions of retirement readers through seven books, twelve guides, and over 800 articles. In addition to his own writings, he frequently appears in major business media outlets such as the Wall Street Journal, USA Today, CNBC, MarketWatch, Investor's Business Daily, New York Times, and more.

As a former social worker turned money manager and author, he has found that retirement is among the most fascinating, yet least understood, phases of life. As a result, he has developed a powerful message to tackle the mental, social, spiritual, and financial aspects of retirement.

All of his work reflects his ground-breaking efforts to challenge the status quo of traditional retirement planning and help people create a No-Regrets Retirement Plan!

Robert has been a speaking and teaching financial and non-financial retirement based programs for over 20 years. His presentations are ideal for every group, from business owners and executives to employees, associations, retirees, and churches.

His conversational and humorous style allows his audiences to get educated in an entertaining way as he creates a memorable experience that touches both the mind and heart. With thought-provoking insights, vivid stories, and a frequent dose of humor, he reaches audiences in a way they do not forget.

Robert has garnered a unique look at wealth and retirement by not only working closely with his own clients for the last twenty years, but also by interviewing numerous celebrities, entertainers, and athletes including Pastor Rick Warren, Deion Sanders, John Sally, Gymnast Shannon Miller, Golfer Annika Sorenstam, Singer Amy Grant, HGTV's the Property Brothers, Pawn Star Rick Harrison, Cheech & Chong, Impersonator Rich Little and more.

He is the founder of the Wealth & Wellness Group, Certified Professional Retirement Coach Designation, and RetirementProject.org. He holds several designations including Certified Kingdom Advisor, Accredited Asset Management Specialist, Certified Mutual Fund Counselor, Chartered Retirement Planning Counselor, and Certified Retirement Coach. He also serves as an expert witness and consultant to attorneys, providing courtroom testimony and litigation support on investment matters.

Robert is married to his amazing wife Amie and together they have a blended family of four wonderful children. Connor, Ava, Luke, and Drake. You can learn more about him at RobertLaura.com

www.ingramcontent.com/pod-product-compliance
Lightning Source LLC
Chambersburg PA
CBHW060602030426
42337CB00019B/3584